W9-AGN-849

Why
Do People Harm
Animals?

Chris Mason

RAINTREE
STECK-VAUGHN
PUBLISHERS

A Harcourt Company

Austin   New York
www.raintreesteckvaughn.com

Published by Raintree Steck-Vaughn Publishers, an imprint of Steck-Vaughn Company

Library of Congress Cataloging-in-Publication Data

Mason, Chris.
   Why do people harm animals? / Chris Mason
   p. cm. -- (Exploring tough issues)
Includes bibliographical references and index.
Summary: Discusses varying opinions on ways in which humans may hurt animals by raising them for food, using them as entertainment, and even keeping them as pets.
   ISBN 0-7398-4962-X
   1. Animal welfare--Juvenile literature. 2. Human-animal relationships--Juvenile literature. [1. Animal welfare. 2. Human-animal relationships.] I. Title. II. Series.

HV4708 .M366 2002
179'.3--dc21   2001048370

Printed in Italy. Bound in the United States.
1 2 3 4 5 6 7 8 9 0 06 05 04 03 02

Picture acknowledgments
The publisher would like to thank the following for their kind permission to use their pictures: AKG Berlin, 8; Associated Press, (cover) (Great Falls Tribune), 35 (Michel Euler), 39 (Denis Poroy), 43 (Louise Buller); Camera Press, 4 (Brian Snyder), 16 (J. Kopec), 33 (bottom) (Darren Regnier); James Davis Travel Photography, 18; Durrell Wildlife Conservation Trust, 37; Ecoscene, (contents) (bottom) (Michael Gore), 7, 26 (Sally Morgan), 34 (Michael Gore); Family Life Pictures, 19 (top) (Angela Hampton); FLPA, 30 (Terry Whittaker); Robert Harding Picture Library, 20 (bottom) (R. Maisonneuve), 25 (Kodak), 36 (bottom), 40 (J. Lightfoot), 44 (Bildagentur Schuster); Hodder Wayland Picture Library, 6 (bottom), 14, 19 (bottom), 20 (top), 21 (Dorian Shaw), 23 (bottom); Impact, 22 (Bruce Stephens), 42 (Philippe Gontier); Panos Pictures, (contents) (top), 17; Popperfoto, (imprint page) (Paul Hackett, Reuters), 10 (John Hrusa, Reuters), 11 (Corinne Dufka, Reuters), 12 (Greg Garay, Reuters), 13 (Andrew Winning), 15 (Jason Reed, Reuters), 24, 32 (Paul Hackett, Reuters); RSPCA Photolibrary, 5, 6 (top), 9 (Philip Meech), 28 (Nathan Strange), 31, 33 (top), 38 (Louise Murray/Wild Images); Science Photo Library, 45 (Simon Fraser); Still Pictures, 27 (Dylan Garcia), 29 (Matthew Wanner), 41 (Peter Weimann); Topham Picturepoint, 23 (top).

Contents

1. How Can People Do That?

What Is Cruelty?

Every year in Canada, more than 250,000 seals are killed for their meat, fur, and other body parts. Most of the seals, many of them cubs, are clubbed to death. Activists around the world have protested this hunt, or "harvest," as the sealers prefer to call it. "Stop this cruelty!" say the campaigners. But it doesn't stop, because not everyone agrees that the hunt is cruel or should end. The Canadian government says that there are plenty of seals, that the hunt is properly controlled, and that the hunters do their best to avoid inflicting unnecessary pain. Who is right?

Arriving at an answer to this question can be difficult, since individuals will always believe that their opinion

> "I think that the worst kind of cruelty is being unfair to animals when you're fed up with them and can't be bothered. If you have a pet, you have to realize how you've got to change when you get one."
>
> *George Cooper, age 12, who has a wire-haired fox terrier, Bob*

◄ *A seal hunter raises a club to beat a seal unconscious during the annual Canadian seal hunt. Seals are killed in this way for their skins.*

or answer is the right one. However, we can all agree on one thing: animals are, for the most part, defenseless creatures when it comes to actions that humans may take against them.

Most of you who read this book will answer these questions in a similar way. Of course we all sometimes say or do something that is cruel, but most people do not intend to be cruel. Most people learn that cruelty causes pain and suffering and come to regret acting cruelly, whether it is to other people or to animals.

Some people, however, are cruel to animals. Governments and charities around the world work hard to protect animals, and yet hundreds of thousands of cases of cruelty to animals are reported every year. Why is this?

▲ *This pony in England was left to starve to death by his owners. Luckily an animal charity, the RSPCA (Royal Society for the Prevention of Cruelty to Animals), rescued him. This is how he looked after several weeks of care and attention.*

Why Are People Cruel to Animals?

Cases of cruelty include people mistreating their pets, people neglecting their animals, farm animals being caused unnecessary suffering, and deliberate acts of cruelty by those who want to inflict misery on animals for fun.

Some people who are cruel to animals do not mean to be so. They do not know or understand what they are doing. Many people cause pain and suffering to their pets because they don't know how to look after them properly. There is no excuse for keeping as a pet an animal that you cannot or do not know how to take care of properly.

▲ *A solitary bear reaching out from its cage at a zoo in Borneo. Large animals like this seem unhappy living in such cramped conditions.*

◀ *This fisherman is sorting a catch of fish from a trawler. Are fishing and hunting examples of cruelty to animals?*

Others do not believe that what they are doing is cruel. For example, hunters and fishermen do not believe that they are being cruel to animals. They often argue that what they do is part of the "natural order" of things.

So why are people cruel to animals? Can we agree on what is cruel and what isn't? Can we stop people from being cruel? To answer these questions we need to know more. This book will provide you with information that will help you find your own answers.

▼ *Pilot whales are hunted and killed for their meat by people living in the Faeroe Islands. The whale hunt is an essential part of their culture.*

case study · case study · case study · case study · case study

Every year the people of the Faeroe Islands in the North Atlantic carry out the *Grindadrap*, the hunting and killing of up to 1,500 pilot whales, which has been a tradition for hundreds of years. The whales are driven to the shore by powerboats and then killed with special long knives. Opponents of the hunt say that it is barbaric. Leivur Janus Hansen, a Faeroese, says, "What do you think is more humane: to have an animal living in a cage all of its life, or to let it roam free from birth to death? Do you think that going to the clean, disinfected supermarket for your meat is more natural than a bloody and messy hunt?"

2. Caring for Animals

People and Animals

People and animals have always interacted. Early humans hunted animals for food, but they soon learned that it was sometimes easier to raise their own animals that could be killed for food. We do not know when people first started keeping animals as pets or companions, but much ancient artwork shows what seems to be tame dogs and cats.

The ancient Egyptians kept and even worshiped cats. The goddess Bastet (sometimes called Pasht) was pictured with a cat's head. The Egyptians mourned the death of a cat and surrendered the city of Pelusium to the Persians to save hundreds of hostage cats that the Persian army had captured. Egyptians law mandated punishments for those who harmed or killed cats.

In the modern age in the United States and Great Britain, the movement to recognize animal rights dates to the early 19th century. At that time, some people began to be concerned about the mistreatment of domestic and farm animals, especially horses, which acted as transportation, beasts of burden, and to power machinery.

▼ *An American coal miner photographed with a pit pony in the 19th century. The animals had to endure very harsh working conditions underground.*

This concern led to the creation of such organizations as the American Society for the Prevention of Cruelty to Animals (ASPCA) and the Royal Society for the Prevention of Cruelty to Animals (RSPCA) in Great Britain.

These organizations hired trained inspectors to investigate and prosecute cases of cruelty to animals. They also established clinics for sick and abandoned animals. Today, both organizations continue to stress the importance of education in stopping cruelty. They provide materials to teachers and children to teach them about the humane treatment of animals.

▼ *An RSPCA inspector examines a pet rabbit. Animal welfare charities such as the RSPCA help teach people how to treat animals responsibly.*

FACT:
The American Society for the Prevention of Cruelty to Animals was founded in 1866 in the United States. It is the oldest American animal rights organization. Today, the ASPCA focuses on national education programs and the creation of shelters for unwanted cats and dogs. It also lobbies to create legal protection for animals. In most places in the United States, animals have only very limited legal rights and are usually defined as a kind of property.

Caring for Animals

In 1917 Maria Dickin set up PDSA (the People's Dispensary for Sick Animals) in Whitechapel, then a very poor part of London's East End. She was shocked by the suffering of the animals belonging to poor people who could not afford to pay for veterinary treatment. She opened a small clinic that offered free medical care for animals.

▼ *Helpers release some of the African penguins that were cleaned up after an oil spill in June 2000 off Cape Town, South Africa. The birds were coated with fuel that leaked from a damaged oil tanker.*

PDSA now runs 45 PetAid animal hospitals throughout Britain. These hospitals treat about 1.3 million pets a year. The charity still offers free veterinary care to pet owners who cannot afford to pay for the necessary treatment.

case study · case study · case study · case study · case study

In June 2000 a massive oil spill off Cape Town, South Africa, threatened tens of thousands of African penguins on Robben and Dassen Islands. Among the volunteers who helped with rescuing and washing the affected birds were many students from local schools. Younger children like Rachel (8) and Shannon Bernhardt (11) and their friend Kaya Kuhn (8) produced a newsletter, "Penguin Post," and organized collections of money to help the rescue effort, along with toothbrushes and towels for cleaning oil off the birds.

PDSA also recognizes the need to educate young people and runs Pet Protectors, a club that teaches children about responsible pet ownership. Young people in their teens also support the organization's work through the PDSA Youth Challenge.

The International Fund for Animal Welfare (IFAW), which is based in the United States, uses protest and publicity to campaign against cruelty to animals. It has campaigned against the annual Canadian seal hunt, whaling, fox-hunting, and the ivory trade.

IFAW concentrates on opposing the killing of wild animals, such as whales and elephants, for commercial profit; protecting the habitat of wild animals; and rescuing animals in distress following natural or people-made disasters, such as oil spills.

"It's time to say enough and insist that our coastlines, their communities, and the animals that live there are properly protected." *Sarah Scarth, IFAW's Emergency Relief Coordinator, after a large oil spill off the South African coast*

▼ *A huge pile of confiscated ivory is burned by an officer of the Kenya Wildlife Service.*

Animals That Help People

▼ *Sue-Ellen Lovett with her seeing-eye dog during the Sydney 2000 Paralympic Torch Relay in Australia.*

Many animals, whether they are domesticated or wild, help people. Seeing-eye dogs for the blind and those used in search and rescue missions are obvious examples. People who work with and keep horses will often talk about how the animal has helped them at important times. There are many true stories of dolphins rescuing or helping people at sea.

In many different cultures, tales of animals with magical powers that help people are common. For example, West African legends tell how fish help to find water during a drought. A well-known Russian story tells of an old wolf that kept a dying man company in Russia. Native Americans have many stories about the special bonds between people and the animals around them.

It seems that people today have lost some of the respect for animals that these ancient stories communicate.

Animals are now often used in therapy to help people who are ill or disabled. Health professionals have come to realize that contact with animals can aid recovery or development. In the United States there are over 2,500 programs that use animals in this way.

At the Cape Cod Therapeutic Riding Center in Massachusetts, children with disabilities can work with different animals. A horse named Pete is just one of those therapeutic animals. He is particularly sensitive to the needs of children who have either Down's syndrome or cerebral palsy, compensating for their poor balance or lack of control. No one at the center doubts the benefits to the children of riding Pete.

▲ *A two-year-old child with learning difficulties closes his eyes as a dolphin in an aquarium in Mexico nudges him gently. This is part of a type of therapy aimed at stimulating the child's brain.*

3. Pets—Companions or Victims?

What Do Pets Mean to Us?

People in the United States will spend about $29 billion on their pets in the year 2001. This amount, which is more than the governments of some poorer countries spend in total, shows how important pets, or what some people call companion animals, are in countries like the United States and Great Britain.

Most pets are no longer just fed scraps. Pet owners can now buy "gourmet" and "diet" products for their pets. People can even buy jewelry and small coats for their dogs or cats. In some places in the United States, people can buy health insurance for their pets to cover the cost of veterinary care.

▼ *People around the world love their pets, but some owners do not think enough about the needs of the animals themselves before taking them home.*

Pets are found in more than 60 percent of the households in the United States. In Britain there are 7.5 million pet cats, 7 million pet dogs, 1 million pet rabbits, and hundreds of thousands of smaller pet animals, such as fish and rodents. Most of these pets are well cared for and happy with their owners.

Sometimes, though, it seems that the way in which we show love for our pets does them more harm than good. A growing number of dogs and cats are treated by veterinarians for being overweight; their owners feed them too much and exercise them too little.

Some animals that we keep as pets are really not suited to living with people. Rabbits do not like being handled and prefer fresh air to life indoors. Goldfish are very sensitive to noise; a tap on their tank can terrify them. Hamsters like to live in holes and become so distressed when handled that they can suffer heart attacks.

When we buy a pet, we often consider our own enjoyment more than the animal's welfare.

▲ *Each year, more and more money is spent on pampering pets—sometimes with the strangest results! This poodle is taking part in a dog-grooming show in Bangkok, Thailand.*

FACT:
A recent survey of pet owners in the United States found that 28 percent talk to pets on their telephones, 27 percent celebrate their pets' birthdays with parties, and 37 percent carry pictures of their pets in their wallets.
PetsMart, 2000

Should We Keep Exotic Pets?

Some people like to keep what are called "exotic pets." These unusual animals, such as spiders, snakes, turtles, and even monkeys and large wild cats, can be very difficult to look after. They often come from habitats very different from ours. They may need special conditions and to be fed food, sometimes other live animals, that comes from their natural homeland.

Many owners of exotic pets take good care of their animals, but some find the responsibility too great. Snakes, in particular, which require live food and grow quite big, are often abandoned by their overwhelmed owners.

▼ *This owner keeps a very unusual mixture of pets; this group includes a dog, a warthog, and a lioness.*

The trade in exotic pets is growing, even though much of it is illegal. Animals that are rare, even those that are facing extinction, often become popular with collectors. People earn a lot of money by capturing and selling rare monkeys, reptiles, wild cats, and birds to collectors in other countries.

International law forbids commerce in endangered animals, and governments and customs officials work hard to stop the trapping and smuggling of them. Despite such efforts, however, animals continue to be trapped, and many of them die while being transported to other countries, packed into unsuitable boxes and crates where they suffocate or starve.

▲ *A variety of small mammals are crammed into cages at an animal market in Quanzhan, China.*

case study · case study · case study · case study · case study

In 1995 customs officers in the Philippines discovered two drills, rare rain forest monkeys from Africa, in a smuggled shipment of exotic pets bound for collectors in Asia. Animal welfare agencies, with the help of the Philippines government, the airline Lufthansa, and the oil company Mobil, organized their return to a refuge in Nigeria—some 8,000 miles (13,000 km) away.

Within a year, the drills were ready for release back into the wild. To the surprise and pleasure of everyone involved, one of the drills gave birth just before her release.

4. On the Farm

Feeding the World

There are more people on Earth than ever before. Since 1960 the world population has doubled. It now stands at over 6 billion. Most of these people, particularly those who live in towns and cities, rely on farmers to feed them.

People who live in richer countries such as Great Britain, Canada, and the United States eat more meat, particularly "fast food" such as hamburgers and fried chicken, than ever before. This trend is spreading to other countries, such as India, where U.S.-owned fast food companies are opening outlets. When people buy meat in supermarkets or meals at fast food restaurants, they expect it to be cheap. If it is not, they go somewhere else. It is only natural that farmers and ranchers try to meet the increased worldwide demand for meat.

FACT:
Every year over 100 million pigs are raised in the United States. Sometimes up to 10,000 pigs are kept in one huge building.
FactoryFarming.com; and The News & Observer, *Raleigh, North Carolina, February 1995*

▼ *Food stands like this cater to people who want their food fast and cheap.*

Most meat-eating Europeans and North Americans expect to be able to buy reasonably priced beef, lamb, chicken, and pork, as well as milk from cows and eggs from chickens. The supermarkets that most people buy from are part of a huge and complex industry.

The farms that produce most of these animals are not like the picture that many of us have of a farm: a few small buildings and barns, some fields, a herd of 20 to 30 cows, a duck pond, and chickens roaming in the farmyard. To meet the growing demand for cheap meat and to make a profit, farms have now become what are called factory farms: huge businesses with hundreds or thousands of animals in pens being raised in "factory units." The more animals there are in a "unit," the more efficient the farm will be, and the more money it will make.

▲ *Many modern farms exist to produce meat for sale in butcher shops.*

▼ *Not all farms look like this; many are run more like industrial factories.*

Factory or Free-Range?

Many people believe that factory or intensive farming—where animals are raised in ways that get the most meat, milk, or eggs from them —is cruel. Cows, which have a natural lifespan of 20 to 25 years, may now produce 40 percent more milk than 20 years ago, but they do not live for more than 5 years before being sent to slaughter.

Hens raised in battery cage systems live four in a cage with a floor the size of a piece of writing paper. They cannot flap their wings or exercise their legs. The windowless shed in which they live may hold up to 90,000 other birds. The European Union (EU) is now phasing out battery production and replacing it with intensive systems that allow the birds more space and some freedom.

▲ *Chicks raised in a battery-type poultry house are tipped out from boxes onto the floor of the unit.*

◄ *Intensive methods of farming mean that many routine operations on the farm, such as delivering feed to the animals, are now mechanized.*

Because many people think that this kind of intensive rearing is cruel, a growing number of farmers are turning to free-range farming. In this system, the animals have much more room when they are kept indoors and are allowed to roam around more when they are outside.

Though they are kept on perches in barns, often in large numbers, free-range chickens are able to move freely both within the barn and outdoors. They can behave as birds naturally do—dust-bathing, stretching, and flapping their wings.

The RSPCA has established a set of guidelines for farmers and retailers, called the Freedom Food Scheme, that helps to encourage this cruelty-free approach to animal rearing.

▲ *Free-range ducks and chickens, such as these birds seen in a farmyard, enjoy much better living conditions than poultry kept in battery cages.*

"We give our animals good home-grown food, plenty of fresh air, roomy and well-bedded winter quarters, and as short a journey to market as possible because we want them to live as well as they can without stress or suffering."
Ruth and Mike Downham, organic farmers in Cumbria, Great Britain

Farming the Seas

Many people see fish farming, or aquaculture, as a way of meeting our food needs without cruelty. Fish farming has been practiced for centuries in Asia and parts of Africa. The new farms, though, are larger and more intensive, like land-based factory farms.

Instead of being caught in the wild, sea fish and shellfish, such as salmon and shrimp, and freshwater fish, such as trout and tilapia, are raised in floating pens fixed to the river or sea bed. The fish are bred in hatcheries and then raised in larger pens where they are fed special food. When they are fully grown, the fish can be easily removed from the pens, killed, and sold.

Aquaculture now produces about one-quarter of the world's fish supply. If you have eaten salmon, shrimp, or trout recently, the chances are that it was raised on a fish farm.

FACT:
Fish farming is one of the fastest-growing agricultural industries in the world. One in five fish eaten by people is produced in a fish farm.
Food and Agriculture Organization of the United Nations

◀ *A salmon hatchery in the highlands of Scotland —once the young fish have hatched, they are reared in pens until they are ready to be killed and eaten.*

Some people feel that fish farming can be cruel. Salmon are carnivores, which means that they eat other marine animals. When they are raised in captivity, they have to be fed food made from other fish and shellfish. It can take up to 11 pounds (5 kg) of wild fish to raise 2.2 pounds (1 kg) of farmed fish. Tilapia and some other freshwater fish do not need animal-based feed; they survive on a more sustainable plant-based diet.

The pens produce pollution from uneaten food, fish waste, and the chemicals used to treat the fish. This pollution can affect other animals. The main worry is that the fish are crowded into the pens and enjoy none of the freedom of movement that a wild fish has. The crowding can be a particular problem at feeding time or when the fish are moved and can lead to distress, injury, and death.

▲ *Wild salmon are naturally strong and vigorous fish; those bred in fish farms have to survive in cramped conditions.*

◀ *Not all the fish on the fishmonger's slab come from the open seas; up to 20 percent of them are likely to have been reared on fish farms.*

5. Animals on Show

All the Fun of the Circus?

Many young people first see large animals, such as tigers, bears, and elephants, in circuses. There's no doubt that many children are excited and happy to see, smell, and hear animals that they have only previously encountered on television or in films or books.

Many people, though, feel that making animals perform in circuses is wrong. Elephants in the wild do not stand upright on tubs, wild bears do not ride little bikes, and tigers don't have to jump though flaming hoops. Circus animals have to be trained to do the tricks that people expect to see. Very often the training is cruel and unnatural. When they are not being trained, the animals are kept in cages, enclosures, or traveling wagons that are quite different from their natural environment. The space for the animals is cramped and unpleasant.

▼ *This chimpanzee, dressed up as a soccer player, has been taught to perform tricks.*

To many people, the worst thing about circuses is that they give people false ideas about wild animals. An elephant in a little dress loses its natural dignity. In the wild a female Asian elephant, the type most often used in circuses, may lead a family for decades, ranging over a wide territory and forming deep and caring relationships. Spending a life in chains and performing tricks in front of children is not natural behavior for an elephant.

The supporters of circuses say that at least they allow people to see animals that they would not otherwise see. Their opponents say that rather than having magnificent wild animals treated as performers in a show, it would be better for people not to see them at all.

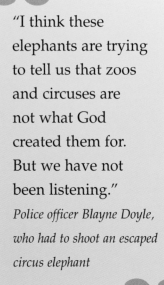

"I think these elephants are trying to tell us that zoos and circuses are not what God created them for. But we have not been listening."
Police officer Blayne Doyle, who had to shoot an escaped circus elephant

◀ *Lots of people enjoy the thrill of seeing wild animals in a circus, but others think that making animals perform like this takes away their natural dignity.*

At the Zoo

The earliest recorded zoo was that of the Queen Hatshepsut of Egypt, who in the 15th century B.C. sent an expedition to the Red Sea to collect exotic animals. Like many of the zoos that were established in the following centuries, Hatshepsut's zoo was created to show off her wealth and power.

The menagerie at the Tower of London, created by King John in the 12th century, was opened to the public in the 17th century. The main attraction was animal baiting (attacks by trained dogs on the chained animals). In 17th-century France, on the other hand, King Louis XIV's zoo was open to scientists for the study of the captive animals.

▼ *The giraffes in London Zoo are kept in large, open enclosures rather than being locked up behind bars in cages.*

The best modern zoos seek to balance entertainment for their customers with the needs and welfare of the animals. Instead of empty cages and ugly pens, the animals live in surroundings that resemble their natural habitats. Sometimes zoos make such realistic habitats to keep their animals happy that visitors cannot always see them! Some zoos have stopped keeping certain animals, such as bears, because it is felt that it is too cruel to keep them penned in captivity.

Zoos also seek to save endangered species by breeding them in captivity and then releasing the animals back into the wild. Some people feel that despite all this good work, zoos are still prisons for animals and that it would be better if more money was spent on protecting them in the wild.

▼ *Some people argue that wild animals, like this rhino, do not belong in a zoo in the center of a city.*

Performing Sea Creatures

A new trend in animal entertainment is the growth of centers and theme parks devoted to sea life. These 21st-century aquariums attract the same type of criticism as zoos because they use captive animals, but they defend themselves by pointing out the high standard of care that they provide for their animals.

Sea Life Centers in Britain are very popular with schools and young people. The "walk through" layout takes visitors past and even under glass tanks that allow them to see marine animals in a version of their natural habitat. The centers are primarily for entertainment, but they also offer a great deal of information and education. The Sea Life Centers do not keep or display larger marine animals as they feel that this would be cruel.

▼ *A killer whale performs for the crowd at the Sea World marine park in San Diego, California.*

The Sea World Adventure Parks in the United States are much larger. Sea World Florida covers several hundred acres and has been home to some of the largest marine mammals, including the famous orca (killer whale), Shamu. Sea World focuses on entertainment, offering rides, shows, and attractions that star 800 different creatures, including whales, walruses, seals, polar bears, sea lions, otters, dolphins, and many others.

▼ *A young boy watches dolphins swim by in a well-lit aquarium tank. Places like this are like underwater zoos.*

Critics of this kind of park say that it is cruel to keep large marine animals captive; they need more space than the park can offer. Sea World says that its animals enjoy their life, are looked after well by experts, and are happy living in the company of others in large tanks. In addition, Sea World is actively involved in education, rescue, rehabilitation, and captive breeding work.

case study · case study · case study · case study · case study

Catharine Mason and her Brownie group visited her local Sea Life Center in Tynemouth, England, for a sleepover:

"It was great, we slept in the hotel next to the center and were allowed in to the center at night. They switched all the lights off except in the tanks—it was beautiful. We learned a lot about fish and they even let us stroke the rays."

6. Hunting and Fighting

Why Watch Animals Fight?

Hurting animals for fun is not as common as it once was. As we study and observe animals more closely, we learn how much they can feel pain and distress.

Badgers, a common animal in England, are rarely seen, because they are so timid. They live in small social groups in underground tunnels called setts. Badger-baiting, in which dogs were set on captured badgers, often already disabled by blows to the head and legs, was once a popular rural activity in Britain. It was made illegal in 1835 as views on animal welfare changed. Badger-baiting is still practiced, however, in great secrecy. London's Metropolitan Police have stated that they fear that it might be on the increase.

▼ These people are watching a cock fight in a market in Thailand. Many bet on the result of the fight in which one of the birds may die.

It is difficult to know why people do things like this. Many spectators like to bet on the outcome of such "fights" between animals, but many who watch just seem to enjoy the bloody spectacle.

Some of the people who take part in badger-baiting would probably enjoy watching a dog fight. This traditional pastime, in which specially bred and trained dogs fight in a ring, has been outlawed in most western countries. Despite the laws forbidding it, there are still many secretly organized fights in Britain, Canada, and the United States. The television channel CNN recently reported its growing popularity in Russia.

As with badger-baiting, betting takes place, but the major enjoyment appears to be from watching the two animals engage in a sickening fight, which usually leaves both badly injured and, quite often, one dead. The RSPCA and ASPCA, which campaign to stamp out dog fighting, often have to treat the injured dogs, which are abandoned by their owners.

The Rights and Wrongs of Fox-Hunting

Fox-hunting with horses and dogs is very much a way of life in the British countryside. Songs and paintings have celebrated it for centuries. For tens of thousands of people, "following the hunt" is part of the traditional New Year festivities.

▼ A huntsman leading his fox hounds during a hunt in England in 1999. When a fox is sighted, the hounds will chase it.

Recently, heated debate has followed efforts in Great Britain by animal rights organizations to have fox-hunting outlawed. Opponents say that it is both cruel and barbaric. They argue that at the beginning of the 21st century we should not permit a sport in which people gain pleasure from watching an animal being torn to pieces by hounds.

Supporters of fox-hunting say that their opponents do not understand traditional country ways. They claim that foxes are a pest that often kill hens, pheasants, and even lambs. Hunting is, they say, a good way of controlling the population of a vicious and destructive animal.

They also argue that the hunts create jobs for people, particularly among those who care for horses. Hunters also argue that they help maintain the countryside by preserving the areas in which they hunt. Fox-hunters are very critical of what they see as the hypocrisy of their opponents, who complain about the killing of a fox but are not concerned about the damage that a fox can do to farm livestock.

▲ *A fox at bay bares its teeth as the hounds close in for the kill at a hunt in Suffolk, England.*

◀ *Hunt saboteurs oppose fox-hunting and attempt to disrupt the hunt and prevent the hounds from finding a fox to chase.*

Killing Animals for Their Skins

Around 40,000 animals a year are trapped for their fur in the United States. The steel-jaw leg traps most commonly used snap shut on a limb, thus breaking or dislocating it. The trapped animal usually survives the initial shock and then suffers agony as it tries to free itself. Some animals have even been known to gnaw through their own legs to break free. Many other animals, which are of no value to the trappers, are also caught in such traps.

The furs or pelts from trapped animals are sold to the fashion industry to be made into coats, wraps, and other items of clothing. A number of animal welfare organizations in the United States are campaigning against this kind of fur trapping. They hope to have the law changed to make it illegal.

▼ *A coyote caught in a leg trap in New Mexico. Traps like this are laid by hunters who catch animals and then sell their skins to the fur trade.*

The annual Canadian seal hunt has caused a huge international outcry, which goes to the heart of the argument about hunting (see also page 4). Every year the Canadian government issues licenses that allow hunters to kill about 250,000 of the population of almost 5 million seals.

"It takes up to 40 dumb animals to make a fur coat. But only one to wear it."
Slogan on a Greenpeace poster opposing the fur trade

People who oppose the hunt say that it should be better controlled or even banned. They believe that the hunters are killing too many seals and that the overall seal population may decline as a result. They are also concerned that the hunt is needlessly cruel— that a more humane method than clubbing seal pups to death can be found.

The hunters say that people are just being sentimental about "cuddly" animals that they know little about.

◄ *Fur is still part of the fashion scene, but many designers now think that wearing animal skins is cruel and outdated.*

7. Losing Natural Habitats

Population Growth and Extinction

When we say that a species of animal has become "extinct," we mean that no more exist in the wild. Extinction can happen naturally. The dinosaurs, for instance, died out because of environmental or climate changes. But humans can cause extinction, too. Some scientists believe that early humans hunted mammoths and mastodons to extinction.

Portuguese sailors and the animals that they introduced to Mauritius hunted the flightless Mauritian dodo to extinction in the 17th century. In North America the passenger pigeon was hunted to extinction through the 19th and early 20th centuries.

▲ *The dodo, a large flightless bird, was hunted to extinction about 350 years ago.*

▼ *Cutting down forests for timber can destroy animals' natural habitats.*

The growing human population is the greatest threat to the animals with which we share the planet. It is not just the number of humans that is to blame, but where humans live and how they live. With over half the human race living in cities, humans constantly require more space for building. Industrial growth and production and new technology require an increased amount of resources.

As humans build on open land, mine for minerals, cut down trees for timber, and turn more land over to farming, they take living space away from wild animals, destroying the habitats that animals need to survive and endangering their continued survival in the wild.

▼ *Jersey Zoo's project to save endangered Mauritius kestrels has been a success.*

case study · case study · case study · case study · case study

Many modern zoos work to protect endangered species. Animals at risk of extinction are bred in zoos and, where possible, released into the wild, thus helping to save them from extinction. The Jersey Zoo in the Channel Islands was one of the first to use this approach, which is called captive breeding. The zoo worked to restore the population in the wild of the Mauritian kestrel, a kind of falcon. Because of the zoo's work, the kestrel population on Mauritius has risen from a low of 4 in the 1970s to more than 800 today.

37

The Threat to Sea Life

The sea might seem to us to be unchanging and safe, so vast that it cannot be harmed. Marine animals are also threatened by habitat loss. Our ports, cities, and factories increasingly pollute coastal areas. Pollution is now so widespread that harmful substances have been found in the flesh of Arctic seals and Antarctic penguins.

▼ *The world under the waves teems with marine life, but even the oceans are being damaged by human activity. Pollution of the sea is now a common problem.*

Whales, especially those that migrate to breed, suffer great harm from human activity. Whales are very sensitive to noise and pollution and will soon leave an area if they are disturbed or upset. Pacific gray whales were once common, but after being hunted nearly to extinction they are now only found in the eastern Pacific. They migrate between their feeding grounds off Alaska in the north to birthing nurseries in the lagoons off Mexico's coast.

▲ *Tourists reach out to touch an adult gray whale at Laguna Ignacio, the place where ESSA's plans to build a salt factory threatened the last undeveloped calving area for the Pacific gray whale.*

When a company called ESSA, jointly owned by the Mexican government and the Japanese firm Mitsubishi, revealed plans to open a salt-manufacturing plant at the lagoons used by the whales to give birth, many people protested. They argued that the noise of pumps and pollution from the plant could drive the whales away. Ships entering and leaving the planned harbor might hit the whales. This loss of habitat was likely to further reduce the gray whale population.

At first ESSA refused to change its plans. But following a worldwide campaign led by Mexican environmentalists, ESSA finally agreed to cancel the plans in order to protect the whales.

Creating Parks for Wildlife

One solution to habitat loss is the creation of national parks. In such areas, development is tightly controlled or even forbidden by law in order to protect natural habitats from human activity.

National parks are now found in countries around the world. What they have in common is that wildlife threatened by human activity finds a refuge there.

Ironically, the parks are becoming victims of their own success. As more and more visitors go to the parks to see "real" nature, they risk damaging the habitats and the animals that live there. For example, there are so many walkers in Britain's Lake District National Park that they are wearing away the vegetation around footpaths. In some U.S. national parks, bears have changed their feeding habits because they have become used to being fed by visitors or stealing from their backpacks.

▶ *A tourist feeds Alpine marmots in Yosemite National Park. Parks allow people to be close to wildlife, but this is not necessarily good for the animals.*

The largest national park in the world is the Qomolongma Nature Reserve in Tibet. The park, which is the size of Denmark, is unusual in that 75,000 people live and work in it. The people who run it feel that the best way to protect endangered species such as snow and clouded leopards is to find ways for humans and animals to live together. Before the reserve was made, uncontrolled logging was destroying the beautiful valleys and the animals that live in them.

By splitting the reserve into zones, some of which allow a certain amount of development, the future of the fully protected areas is guaranteed. The reserve has been so successful that a second larger one, the Four Great Rivers Preserve, is being planned in eastern Tibet.

▲ Snow leopards are rare wild cats that live in the Himalayas. The creation of a huge national park in Tibet has helped to provide a safe home for this endangered species.

8. Ready to Act

Cruelty or Not?

You may have noticed on the labels of some cosmetics or cleaning products the words "Not tested on animals," "Cruelty free," or "Against animal cruelty." Cruelty-free products (as these items are often called) are becoming much more popular as opposition to animal testing grows.

The people who make cosmetics and cleaning products have to be sure that they are safe for people to use; they could, for instance, cause skin rashes or, worse, serious illnesses, such as cancer, if they were sold in shops without first being tested for safety. For a long time scientists have believed that the best way to carry out safety tests is to try the products on animals. Many tests for different products have been carried out in laboratories that use specially bred animals, such as dogs, cats, rats, monkeys, rabbits, and mice for this purpose.

▼ Animals, such as rats, are used in laboratories to test the safety of many household products before they are put on sale to the general public.

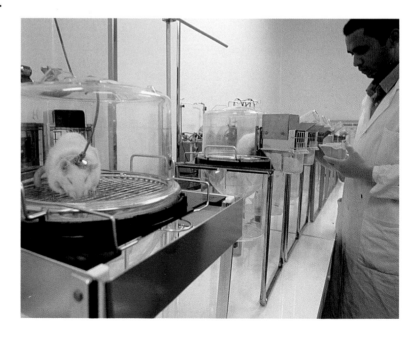

Some of the tests are painful and cause suffering to the animals. They may involve dripping the product onto the animal's eyes or shaven skin, or animals may be force-fed or made to inhale the substance being tested. Many of the tests are for toxicity and cause unpleasant and extreme reactions in the animals.

The scientists who do this work point out that they try hard to minimize suffering and that they are acting for the benefit and safety of us all. Many other people, including other scientists, believe that the tests are cruel and unnecessary. Because of the public outcry, many companies no longer use animal testing. The testing on animals of substances for use in making cosmetics is now illegal in the European Union.

> "To my mind the life of the lamb is no less precious than that of a human being. I should be unwilling to take the life of the lamb for the sake of the human body. I hold that the more helpless a creature, the more entitled it is to protection by man from the cruelty of man."
>
> *Mohandas K. (the Mahatma) Gandhi*

These activists have dressed up in cow costumes to protest the destruction of cattle at risk of infection from "Mad Cow Disease" or BSE (bovine spongiform encephalitis).

43

Protesters and Animal Rights

Animal testing is widely used throughout the world for household products, food additives, alcohol, and other items commonly used in homes, offices, and factories. The most common use of animals for such purposes is in the testing of medical products, especially new drugs. In the United States, laws regulate the conditions under which such testing takes place. Such laws are intended to reduce the amount of needless suffering by the animals.

Opponents of animal testing believe that it should be outlawed completely, even if such testing might result in benefits to humans. They suggest alternatives to animal testing, such as computer modeling and the use of synthetic and cloned human skin for testing new products. Feelings run high in the arguments over this issue.

Huntingdon Life Sciences (HLS), which has its headquarters in Great Britain, is one of the largest companies that use animals for testing and research. Among the products HLS has a role in producing are medicines, agricultural chemicals, and food additives.

▼ *It is easy for people to forget when they put on their lipstick that substances in the product were probably tested on an animal.*

HLS has been targeted often for protests by animal rights activists. The campaigners have tried to discourage investors and customers by generating negative publicity about the company's activities.

Some protesters have sent threats to HLS employees and attacked their property. The company argues that its research ultimately helps save human lives and that it is investigating alternatives to animal testing.

Such arguments about the rights and wrongs of animal testing take us back to the question asked at the beginning of this book: Is it cruel to use animals in this way? This is a question that you must think about carefully and answer for yourself.

▲ *Many supporters of animal testing point out that the trials often help companies to produce life-saving drugs.*

FACT:
In 1999 2,569,295 animals were used in scientific procedures (tests, research, and training) in Great Britain:
63 percent of the animals used were mice, 0.0023 percent were dogs.
64 percent of the procedures were carried out without anesthetic.
20 percent of the procedures were for toxicity and 64.9 percent of the tests were for medical products.
UK Home Office Statistics, 1999

GLOSSARY

Activist
A person who tries, through argument, publicity, and direct action, to persuade people to change their attitude to something.

Ancient Egypt
The civilization based around the Nile River in what is now Egypt, which lasted from about 3000 B.C. until about A.D. 300.

Aquariums
Displays of glass tanks containing fish and other marine and freshwater animals and plants.

Carnivore
An animal that eats meat.

Charities
Organizations that help people or animals in need.

Commercial exploitation
Using something to make a profit.

Companion animals
A term for pets that is growing in popularity because it suggests that pets are not simply the property of their owners.

Domestic, domesticated
Trained or raised to be used to live in homes or in the company of people.

Extinction/extinct
The death of the last member of a species of animal or plant in the wild.

Habitat
The natural surroundings and conditions in which animals and plants live.

Hatchery
A place where eggs are hatched.

Humane treatment
Behavior that is compassionate toward human or animal life.

Intensive units
Places or buildings where as many farm animals as possible are kept.

Ivory trade
The selling of elephant tusks and items made from them.

Mammal
A class of fur- or hair-covered animals that give live birth and suckle their young with milk; includes humans, whales, dogs, and cats.

Mature
Adult or grown-up.

Migrate
To travel long distances, usually in search of warmer weather for feeding or breeding purposes.

Prosecute
To take to court to answer criminal charges.

Refuge
A place of shelter.

Reptiles
A class of animals that includes snakes, crocodiles, and tortoises.

Rodents
An order of small gnawing mammals that includes rats, gerbils, and mice.

Subsidies
Money given by government to support business and industry.

Toxicity
The level of how poisonous something is.

Veterinarian
A person trained in the medical care of animals.

Whaling
The hunting of whales.

FURTHER INFORMATION

BOOKS TO READ

Cohen, Daniel. *Animal Rights: A Handbook for Young Adults.* Brookfield, CT: Millbrook Press, 1993.

Day, Nancy. *Animal Experimentation: Cruelty or Science? (Issues in Focus).* Berkeley Heights, NJ: Enslow Publishers, 2000.

Hanmer, Trudy J. *The Hunting Debate: Aiming at the Issues (Issues in Focus).* Berkeley Heights, NJ: Enslow Publishers, 1999.

Harnack, Andrew (ed). *Animal Rights: Opposing Viewpoints (Opposing Viewpoints Series).* San Diego, CA: Greenhaven Press, 1996.

Owen, Marna A. *Animal Rights—Yes or No (Pro/Con).* Minneapolis, MN: Lerner Publications Company, 1993.

WEBSITES

http://www.peta-online.org/kids/
This web site is designed for children, parents, and teachers. Children can find up-to-date information about animal rights, learn how to take action on animal issues that may be important to them, and join in discussions.

http://www.aspca.org/jfk/
This web site helps kids learn and ask questions about animals, find out more about animal rights, see how much they know about animal trivia, and plenty more!

http://www.animaland.org/
This web site is created by the ASPCA and is designed for younger readers. Children can play games, ask questions, and have a lot of fun while learning.

ORGANIZATIONS

The American Humane
Association
63 Inverness Drive East
Englewood, CO 80112-5117
Tel: 800-227-4645
Tel: 303-792-9900
Fax: 303-792-5333
www.americanhumane.org

The American Society for the
Prevention of Cruelty to
Animals
424 East 92nd Street
New York, NY 10128
Tel: 212-876-7700
e-mail: education@aspca.org
www.ASPCA.org

The Humane Society of
the United States
2100 L Street, NW
Washington, DC 20037
Tel: 202-452-1100
www.hsus.org

The International Fund
for Animal Welfare
Headquarters (USA)
IFAW US
411 Main Street
P.O. Box 193
Yarmouth Port, MA 02675
Tel: 508-744-2000
Fax: 508-744-2009
www.ifaw.org

INDEX